1667 4515

NATIONAL GEOGRAPHIC SOCIETY

DESTINATION
AUSTRALIA

BY JONATHAN GRUPPER

NATIONAL GEOGRAPHIC SOCIETY
WASHINGTON, D.C.

Today, you're not going to believe your own eyes.

Today, you're going to see kickboxing kangaroos and a jellyfish that's bigger than you are. You're going to fly with a sugar glider and swim with a shark. You'll meet emus and echidnas, koalas, crocs, and kookaburras.

Today, you're about to experience a day in the life of a place like no other on Earth. It's called Australia.

Sixty-five million years ago, when the continents were still forming, one drifted far away from the others. Life here was left all to itself, and, over time, it became different. Australia's animals are some of the world's weirdest and most wonderful. And that goes as well for the amazing habitats where they live.

Australia, Northern Territory

Your flashlight's beam bounces off the blue gum trees. Silently, you tiptoe through a mysterious forest paradise. Because it's south of the Equator, Australia is called the land down under. Well, Tasmania is an island off Australia's southeast coast, so you might call it the land down under the land down under!

Suddenly, you stop in your tracks: *Ghhhrruuuur…*

That sound! Is it a monster? No, though it is a devil—a Tasmanian devil. But its growl is worse than its bite, and it usually only eats animals it doesn't have to kill. A sharp cry in the leaves above sends it scurrying.

Look, up in the treetops. Is it a bird? Is it a squirrel? No, it's a sugar glider, and it can launch itself from a branch and then glide half the length of a football field in a single bound. Being airborne keeps it out of that devil's reach.

Imagine being able to jump like that!

Tasmania by Night

Tasmanian Devil

Sugar Glider

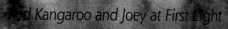
Red Kangaroo and Joey at First Light

Shake the morning dew off your feet. Miles to the north, dawn is breaking across a wide field. And guess who's had grass on their minds all night?

Australia is kangaroo country. In all, there are at least 45 different species of 'roo here. Today, a mob of 50 reds comes hopping along like a small army on pogo sticks. To them, all that grass means breakfast is served.

Look up. Some may be taller than a person. Look down. Your shoe size might be 5. If they wore shoes, theirs would be a size 22. Look fast—they can jump the length of a school bus. Look out! Two males are fighting, putting those oversize feet to the test. To see who's boss, kangaroos kickbox!

Boxing Kangaroos

A Tiny Joey Feeds in Mother's Pouch

But the 'roo's real wonder is in the pocket. Kangaroos are *marsupials*. That means they're mammals, like you are, with a big difference. Females have a pouch, and when a baby kangaroo is no bigger than a jellybean, it crawls up its mother's belly into her fold. There it stays for months until it's big enough to make it on its own.

Animal oddities are Australia's specialty.

A Platypus Shows Off Its Duckbill

Drop behind the reeds and don't make a sound. There, making its way from the river into its burrow—what in the world could it be? It swims and lays eggs. It has fur and a tail like a beaver's. It feeds its young milk like a mammal does but has webbed feet and a bill like a duck's. In fact, the animal is so unusual that when a specimen was first sent back to Europe people thought it must have been sewn together as a hoax!

Yes, the platypus is another mammal—believe it or not, one that lays eggs. That makes it a *monotreme*. There are only three kinds of monotremes on Earth, and two of them are in Australia.

Now you slip into the river as well—in your canoe. As you paddle downstream, the booyong and lillipilly trees give way to dense mangroves. The river gets wider and slower. Emerging slowly out of the muddy water, a pair of eyes stare you down....

Platypus Gliding Through Water

Suddenly, a sea eagle explodes on the scene, dive-bombing before you. The only one more surprised than you is the huge barramundi fish the bird has caught in its powerful talons. But the surprise is on the sea eagle. It bursts into the air as the water erupts with a set of fearsome jaws, hungrily snapping up the prize.

Now you know who belonged to those eyes.

Salties, they're called—the saltwater crocodiles that rule these wetlands. They can grow up to 20 feet long and weigh more than a ton. That's bigger than a car! Better stay clear. Tempers are flaring.

Once the morning is over, for many, so is mealtime.

Crocodile Grabbing a Barramundi Fish

Sea Eagle

The sun is getting higher overhead. Everywhere you look, animals are retreating from its glare. Not so the emu. Perched on his nest, day in, day out, he stays.

So what's a *he* doing nest sitting? Well, eight long weeks ago, mom laid the eggs, and ever since, dad has been patiently tending to them. He hasn't had food or drink—a tall order for an animal this big. At two to three times your weight, the emu is the largest bird on Earth, except for the ostrich. He's so heavy, he can't even fly.

By high noon the emu and his eggs are the only signs of life. It's time to head for the one stretch of Australia that's always bursting with activity.

Emu Nest with Eggs and Chicks

Flippers: check. Air tank: check. Wet suit, weight belt. Tighten that mask. *Kersplash!* Welcome to the Great Barrier Reef, the longest strip of coral reefs on Earth.

What's coral? Swim closer and take a look. The seafloor is crowded with clumps and columns, branches and fans. Are they rocks? Plants? Jewels? No, they're great clusters of tiny, brightly colored animals called coral polyps. Millions upon millions spread side by side to form sprawling undersea colonies along Australia's northeastern shore.

Where there are coral reefs, there are other marine animals in dazzling array. Cuttlefish, sea stars, and a paper nautilus glide past. A fringed sponge crab wears a sea squirt like a hat. Clown anemonefish slip within the tentacles of sea anemones, unharmed by their sting. The coral reef is alive with wonders.

Diver with Cuttlefish;
Aerial View of Great Barrier Reef

Giant Blue Clam with Soft Coral Colony

Firebrick Sea Star

Clown Anemonefish

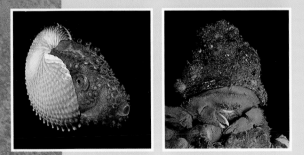

*Paper Nautilus; Fringed Sponge Crab
with Sea Squirt for Hat*

You swim and you swim and, before you know it, you've swum past the reef. Out in the open ocean, you'd better take care. Dangers loom. It's time to climb into a shark cage for protection.

There!—a box jellyfish. Stay in your cage, or else. If you get caught in its tangle of stinging tentacles— each four times your length—you could die within minutes.

There!—a great white. At more than 20 feet long, it's the shark most feared in all the deep.

But then these waters are their home. It's you who are out of place here. Even these creatures can some- how seem less frightening when we stop and admire them for what they are: animals who are simply successful at surviving.

Back ashore, turn in your wet suit for wheels....

Box Jellyfish

Great White Shark

Thorny Devil

Frilled Lizard

mid a sparse woodland, you pull your four-wheel drive over to find the shade of a mulga tree. But look who—or what—you've scared out of hiding!

The frilled lizard is smaller than you are. But in a flash, it turns on you and spreads the enormous flaps on its neck. It opens its mouth wide, making a ferocious spectacle of itself. And now it strikes out with its greatest secret weapon of all...

It runs for its life!

The trees slip away in your rearview mirror. Ahead, all you can see is a wall of wind-blown red sand as your car bounces and bucks, plowing across the vast desert center of the continent.

So this is the outback. Not a soul in sight—except for that strange, armor-plated lizard. A thorny devil slips across a dune. It's as if it knows that something in this outback world is about to change.

few choice times a year it happens, an unexpected drop at a time. The sky opens up. Both you and the outback's dry earth are drenched in a pounding rainstorm.

Stirring underground is a fat water-holding frog. For months, it has stayed in its burrow, encased in hardened mud. Tonight, with the rain, it will venture out to feed and find a mate. In a few days, it will return underground, awaiting the next chance downpour.

The cloudburst sends insects scurrying by the thousands. But on their way, a colony of ants is greeted by the rapid-fire tongue of that thorny devil. And right behind it comes a termite hunter— a spiky ball of an animal called an echidna. Yes, that's the other monotreme that lives in Australia. Like the platypus, it's a mammal that lays eggs!

Water-Holding Frog

Echidna

Storm Threatens Termite Mounds in the Outback

Dingoes Attacking a Lace Monitor

ook fast! Out of nowhere they lunge, snarling and gnashing their teeth—a pair of hungry dogs, known as dingoes. At once, the monitor lizard they're after snaps into action, rearing up and looking mean.

Dingoes are like the dogs you know, except for one thing—they're wild. Around 4,000 years ago they were brought here by sailors from Asia. With little competition from other predators, they had the run of Australia. Dingoes are tough enough to live just about anywhere, from deserts to forestlands.

If only that were true for another Aussie....

Dingo Den with Pups

Koala Snoozes in a Tree

For these cuddly creatures, home is only where the eucalyptus trees grow. Just look at the koalas up there. They grunt. They smell like cough drops. They snooze away 19 hours of the day. Why then, you wonder, are people so in love with koalas? That's easy: They're irresistible.

All day long they've been fast asleep, perched high in the treetops. It's only now, as the sun begins to set, that the koalas begin to stir. For the next five hours they'll eat more than half a pound of eucalyptus leaves. That takes work, and it's not the kind of meal that has much get up and go. It's no wonder koalas have to sleep so much.

Once the coast was rich with the kind of woodlands koalas love. No longer.

Kissing Koalas

Koala, Awake at Last

*hhhhrrrrrmmm!*

A chain saw, the nemesis of the eucalyptus forest! Before another tree falls, you scurry through the bush. But you're in for a surprise. There, twirling its long feathers, is one wild-looking bird—and the song it's singing is the unmistakable roar of a chain saw.

The lyrebird mainly mimics other birds, but it's capable of imitating car engines, horns, even sirens—anything it takes to attract a mate's attention. So far, though, the only one he's attracted is you!

Is that why you now hear laughter rising through the treetops? That's a kookaburra, the loudest beak in the forest. Come sunset, the canopy fills with bird life. Dozens of rainbow lorikeets savor the flowers, their plumage aglow with the dusk.

Another day in Australia is drawing to a close. Last stop: the far west with the sinking sun....

Eucalyptus Forest

Kookaburra

Rainbow Lorikeet

Lyrebird

27

They've done it again. The creatures of the Australian day have fed themselves and their young. They've struggled and somehow survived. Now, for the creatures of the night, a world of opportunities will awaken.

You squint. The last rays of light spread long across the western sky. The sun is announcing its promise. That tomorrow it will return to the animals who count on it.

That their incredible land can await its return and yours as well. Soon enough, you will be back to Australia, sure as the sun.

Kangaroos Hopping Into the Sunset

A Note from the National Geographic Society

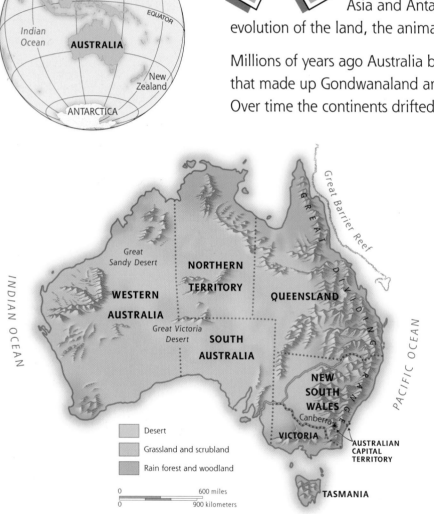

Australia is a mainly arid land with areas of desert, grassland, and scrubland filling its interior. Rain forest and woodland hug much of the coastline, and the Great Barrier Reef stretches for 1,250 miles off the northeastern shore.

Australia may be the smallest and flattest continent on the planet, but it looms large as a land of wonders. Nestled in a southern corner of the globe between Asia and Antarctica, Australia is a place where the evolution of the land, the animals, and the people has been unique.

Millions of years ago Australia belonged to the cluster of continents that made up Gondwanaland and that shared plants and animals. Over time the continents drifted apart inch by inch. Life developed differently in Australia from elsewhere.

Australia's native animals show the impact of their island development. There are three types of mammals in the world. One type is found throughout the world. These are the placentals: mammals that develop inside the mother's body. The other two types—marsupials and monotremes—are found mainly in Australia. Marsupials are pouched mammals, like kangaroos. Marsupial babies begin development inside the mother's body then continue to develop in her external pouch. The monotremes are the most unusual mammals—they hatch from eggs! This group includes the platypus and the echidna.

Not all of Australia's animals are so unusual. When Australia drifted closer to Asia, bats and rats came aboard. Asian settlers brought dingoes about 4,000 years ago. As European settlers came to the continent, they brought animals with them, like camels that arrived in the 1860s and sheep, which now outnumber the human population.

Australians live mostly along the coast where the land is wetter than in the vast, dry interior. The first humans on the continent were the Aborigines, who came over from Asia 50,000 years ago, perhaps more. The first European to discover Australia was Dutchman Willem Jansz in 1606. In 1770 Captain James Cook, a British seafarer, explored the east coast. England began to colonize Australia, slowly at first, then more quickly, developing the continent as a penal colony: a place to send convicted criminals for punishment.

Australia became an independent country in 1901. The people are generally proud of their convict and colonist origins, and the Australian character tends to be adventuresome and unconventional. With rich natural and human resources Australia has grown and modernized rapidly, both from an economic and political standpoint. But as the country develops, respecting and preserving this special continent—and all its inhabitants—is an important national goal.

Uluru, a sacred site for Aborigines, was formerly known as Ayers Rock and is one of Australia's most distinctive geographic landmarks.

This Australian boy, a descendant of European settlers, stands with a camel at one of the large farms called stations.

An Aboriginal boy wears traditional body paint.

Published by the
National Geographic Society
1145 17th St. N.W.
Washington, D.C. 20036

John M. Fahey, Jr.
*President and Chief
Executive Officer*

Gilbert M. Grosvenor
Chairman of the Board

Nina D. Hoffman
Senior Vice President

William R. Gray
*Vice President and Director
of the Book Division*

Staff for this Book

Nancy Laties Feresten
Director of Children's Publishing

Suzanne Patrick Fonda
Editor

Jennifer Emmett
Associate Editor & Project Editor

Jo H. Tunstall
Editorial Assistant

Marianne Koszorus
Art Director

Dorrit Green
Designer

Karen Gibbs
Illustrations Editor

Carl Mehler
Director of Maps

Stuart Armstrong
Map Art

Lewis R. Bassford
Production Manager

Vincent P. Ryan
Manufacturing Manager

FRONT COVER: Bounding gray kangaroos
TITLE PAGE: Wattled cassowary
ENDPAPERS: A mob of red kangaroos

Illustrations Credits

Front Cover Jean-Paul Ferrero/Auscape; back cover (top) Chuck Davis/Tony Stone Images; (bottom left) Mitsuaki Iwago/Minden Pictures; (bottom right) Art Wolfe/Tony Stone Images; endpapers Jean-Paul Ferrero/Auscape; p. 1 Art Wolfe/Tony Stone Images; pp. 2–3 Mitsuaki Iwago/Minden Pictures; pp. 4–5 Melinda Berge; p. 5 (left) Shin Yoshino/Minden Pictures; p. 5 (right) Australasian Nature Transparencies; p. 6 Mitsuaki Iwago/Minden Pictures; p. 7 (top) Australian Picture Library; (bottom) Mitsuaki Iwago/Minden Pictures; p. 8 Animals Animals/Gerard Lacz; pp. 8–9 D. Parer & E. Parer-Cook/Auscape; pp. 10–11 (both) Belinda Wright; pp. 12–13 Fred Bavendam/Minden Pictures; p. 14 Fred Bavendam/Minden Pictures; pp. 14–15 Paul Chesley/Tony Stone Images; p.15 (all) Fred Bavendam/Minden Pictures; p. 16 David Doubilet; pp. 16–17 Chuck Davis/Tony Stone Images; pp. 18–19 Mitsuaki Iwago/Minden Pictures; p. 19 Belinda Wright; p. 20 (top) D. Parer & E. Parer-Cook/Auscape; (bottom) Mitsuaki Iwago/Minden Pictures; pp. 20–21 Earth Scenes/Michael Fogden; pp. 22–23 (all) Jean-Paul Ferrero/Auscape; p. 24 Paul McKelvey/Tony Stone Images; p. 25 (top) Art Wolfe/Tony Stone Images; (bottom) David Barnes/Tony Stone Images; p. 26–27 Mitsuaki Iwago/Minden Pictures; p. 27 (top) John Cancalosi/Auscape; (center) Mitsuaki Iwago/Minden Pictures; (bottom) Zefa Picture Library; pp. 28–29 Mitsuaki Iwago/Minden Pictures; p. 31 (top) Art Wolfe/Tony Stone Images; (left) Medford Taylor; (right) Doug Armand/Tony Stone Images; p. 32 Mitsuaki Iwago/Minden Pictures.

To my father, who read to me at bedtime.

National Geographic would like to thank Dr. Angus Martin, a consultant with the Melbourne Zoo, and Kathryn Berg, with the Royal Geographical Society of Queensland, for reviewing the manuscript and illustrations and providing helpful comments. The author is grateful to Celia Carey for her research assistance.

Library of Congress
Cataloging-in-Publication Data
Grupper, Jonathan.
    Destination : Australia / by Jonathan Grupper.
       p. cm.
    Summary: Describes the characteristics of some of Australia's unusual animals, including the kangaroo, platypus, echidna, lyrebird, and koala.
    ISBN 0-7922-7165-3
    1. Zoology—Australia—Juvenile literature. [1. Zoology—Australia.]   I. Title.
QL338.G756   2000
591'.994—dc21   99–29944

A red kangaroo takes a breather.

JAN 2001